LEGAL OBLIGATIONS FOR TAXING FREELANCE WORK

VOLUME 2, ISSUE 2 OF BRILLOPEDIA

ANUSHKA KUMAR

Contents

Preface   *v*

Publication   *vii*

1. Abstract   1

2. What Is A Freelance Work?   2

3. Steps For Taxing Freelance Work   4

4. Conclusion   8

Preface

"Start writing, no matter what. The water does not flow until the faucet is turned on".

-Louis L'Amour

Hundreds of students and professors are contributing their work to Brillopedia, we are here to provide ample information about Law and Contemporary issues. Our aim is to provide a platform for today's generation to express their views and ideas on law and contemporary law.

Publication

This research paper is published in volume 2, issue 2 of Brillopedia

ABSTRACT

The potential of human mind to crave freedom, and break the paradigm of the social stigma in the process, never fails to impress. After generations working a 9 to 5, the time has come for the working class to prioritise their mental and manual skills over a constant cash flow acquirement. Freelance work is one such step.

Not everyone idolises strict working hours and rigid working scope of work. Freelance acts as a platform for these people to form contract based relationship with their clients and earn through their skill and expertise, without having to commit to a single client or corporation in their entirety and work on their behalf. Freelancers have the freedom of choosing their clients, their work of place, working hours, decide their pay rate etc.

However, there exists a much significant distinction when taxing obligations are concerned. Since the scope of working and the involvement of the clients differs when it comes to freelance work, the legal formalities as well differ in some areas.

This article aims to focus on step by step fulfilling of taxing obligations for freelancers and make the readers understand each and every aspect to it. In the end the reader would get full knowledge about the procedure of taxing a freelancer, and what differences it has with other job types. This article covers all the important sections of The Income Tax act, 1961 and form related to filing for income tax returns.

CHAPTER TWO

WHAT IS A FREELANCE WORK?

Freelance is a contract based profession, wherein a person instead of indulging into the stereotypical 9 to 5 job, offers his services and skills to the client. The income tax laws of India state that freelancing incomeis, any income which is earned either by the intellect or physical ability of a person, and such income is said to bemade from a profession and will be put in the category of income from "Profits and gains from business and profession" and will be taxed accordingly. Freelancers will notbe a known as a company employee or even get listed. Any benefits (such as PF)from the Company Law, will not be received by them. There is also absolutely no obligation to visit the office or designated place of working. The freelancer just needs to complete the work by the (pre-agreed) deadline. Since there are manypeople who do not prefer a 9 to 5 job, freelancing work is the best option for them. Freelancing isan efficient way of working, both for the company and the freelancer. However, income earnedthrough the freelancing work shall be liable for taxation if it fits the category, as set by thetaxation laws.

Any income earned by someone by offering up their intellectual or manual skills is considered incomefrom work, according to the income tax laws of India. Such income is liable for tax andwill be considered under the head of "Profit and Gains from Business or Profession". Thetotalincome gets calculated by the addition of all receipts received while the job was being done. Bank accountstatement of freelancers is a document they can rely on to get this information, as long as they receive all oftheir professional income through bank channels.

With the evolution and growth of internet and technology, freelancing has also become a lucrative earning path, for those who wish to earneither part time or full time income. Theincome of the freelancers and bloggers, comes through various sources which might include sales, advertisements, offering services like web designing etc.

• 3 •

STEPS FOR TAXING FREELANCE WORK

<u>Gross Income</u>

The income of the Freelancer is taken under the income head "Profit and gains from business and profession".The first step for filing the income tax returns is to calculate the total gross income during the financial year. Now as most of the times the payment to a freelancer is done online, it is rather easy for the professional to calculate his or her gross income.

The gross income is calculated for a given financial year, i.e. from 1st of April, tothe 31stof March of the next year. Loans taken do not count as an income.

<u>Deduction of the Expenses</u>

All the expenses of the financial year which a freelancer makes towards the business areto be deducted from the gross annual income. The tax rates are applicableonly on the profits.The business expenses can be in various forms, such as internet chargesor expenses related to purchasing equipments etc. For instance, a software developer, who works as a freelancer, can deductthe expenses which he made towards software purchases or for testing an Android application, whenhe makesit.

Some expenses, which fall under the category of both personal and business purpose(like internet), the taxing authorities will have to see the consumption monthly and the payment patterns, and assign areasonable percentage towards the business (or deduction) purpose.

<u>Depreciation Deductions</u>

A freelancer must deduct all the expenses which relate to depreciation, from the net annualturnover, or the gross income. Every year the equipment usedundergowear and tear, and their valueconsequently decreases.The decrement in the amount of the equipment is known as depreciation. Photographers for example, can calculate thedepreciation accumulated towards the cameras, and the equipments used for printing. Web developers candenote the depreciation which they incur towards the laptops, and other devices andgadgets that they use in getting the work done.

Depreciation is an economically viable way to spread the cost of a particular asset over a period of time, rather than reflecting costs in the past, as these gadgets are used for a long time.

If someone is working in a rented place, they can apply for exemption for rent. Fees payable for obtaining or holding a membership of a professional association, as well as business registration, are also exempt from paying taxes. Therefore, all costs incurred by a freelancer for business purposes are tax-free. Expenses should be legal, and should not be done for personal purposes.

Include Income from All Other Sources

Apart from the income which a person makes from freelancing, he/she should also include otherincomes earned through other sources in the ITR. Some of these incomes include:

- Profits made by property, in the form of a sales profit, or a rental return
- Income from the savings account, or Fixed Deposit, in the form of interest.
- Revenue from stock trading, equity, etc.
- All other types of income generated.
- Any income earned by working overtime, from the employer, in that year.
- Any other income not mentioned here.

Deductions/ Tax Exemptions Under the Section 80 of Income Tax Act, 1961.

- Section 80C

This section provides a deduction of up to Rs 1.5 Lakhs, for payments made towards the life insurance policies,provident fund, tuition fees, buying or building of any residentialproperty/fixed deposits etc.

- Section 80 CCC

It provides tax deductions for investments made towards the pension plans. The maximum exemption limitis set to Rs 1.5 lakhs.

- Section 80 CCD

Exemptions can be claimed towards investment made in the Central Government Pension Schemes. If theinvestment made does not increases 10% of the salary of the individual, then the contribution of both the employer and taxpayer, would be exempted from taxation.

- Section 80 D

Under this section, expenses made towards the payment of premiums of the health insurancepolicies are exempted. The freelancer can also buy the policy for their spouse or child, and claim thedeductions.

- Section 80 DD

This section offers deductions towards treatment of normal and severe disabilities, which cango up to Rs 1.25 lakhs.

- Section 80 DDB

Offers Exemption towards treatment of certain specified diseases.

- Section 80 E

Deductions for loan taken for educational purposes.

- Section 80 EE

The Section is for individuals exclusively, and exempts the payments made towards a loan, forpurchasing a property for residential purposes.

- Section 80 G

The Section provides up to a 100% deduction for the donations made to the charitable funds,including the Prime Minister Relief Fund, and the

National Defense Fund among others.

Credit the TDS Deductions

All the income which a freelancer earns, after the TDS has been deducted from it, is useful towards exemptions. The clients usually deduct the TDS when they makepayments to a freelancer. A claim can be made for the TDS for freelancer's deductions, when filing theITR form, and save good amounts of money.The freelancer can use the Form 26 AS for this purpose. The form is linked to the PAN number, and helps the freelancer know all the TDSthat has been deducted. While filing the ITR, the freelancer has to be sure to include all the deductions.

Advance Tax

When the cumulative tax liability of a freelancer is more than Rs 10,000, he or she may berequired to pay the Advance Tax. When taxes are paid at frequent intervals, instead of all at once during the year, then this process is called as Advance Taxation. If someone fails to paythis tax, there would be an interest charged on the final tax account, under the Section 234 B, and234 C, of the Income Tax Act.

Presumptive Taxation

Freelancers can use the Presumptive Taxation method, and break free from the tiring task ofaccount bookkeeping, when the income earned by them is less than Rs 50 Lakhs during the givenfinancial year.

The program was initially available only to entrepreneurs/businessmen, but is now expanding to include freelancers as well. Taxes are charged @ 8% of the total gross annual income of the entrepreneur. For example, if a businessman earns a profit of Rs 100, he can say Rs 8 as profit.

The new section 44ADA, inserted in the 44AD of the Income Tax Act, brings the professionals into the ambit of tax relief. The presumptive assumption charge is 50% for freelancers. Therefore, for a turnover of Rs 100, the profit will be taken as Rs 50.

Income Tax Taxation Slabs

The same taxation slabs, which apply to the rest 9 to 5 class is applied to the freelancing individuals as well. Incomes up to Rs 2.5 lakhsare not taxed upon, income between 2.5 lakhs to 5 lakhs are taxed @ 10%, 5 lakhs to 10lakhs @ 20%, and above 10 lakhs @30%. The freelancers calculate income tax as per these tax rates only.

CONCLUSION

To conclude, it is clear that there exists a slight yet significant distinction when it comes to taxing a freelancer.Freelance work has a rather bright futuristic characteristic to it, hence it is important to understand the distinctions which it has from regular jobs, to understand this segment of economy even in more depth. The complex Indian taxation laws are very specific and have a to the point remedy for each andevery occupation. The freelancing sector is rising day by day and might have a scope for taxevasions as there is a few percentages of employers and employees who do not keep theirmodestly up to date when it comes to tax liabilities. However, the stringent and diverse Indiantaxation structure makes it easy for the authorities to compute taxes within an organized ambitand structure.